DISCERNING THE SPIRITUAL CLIMATE OF YOUR CITY

A guide to understanding spiritual mapping

Alice Smith

© Copyright 2018 Alice Smith
Formerly titled, *Discerning the Climate of The City*, Copyrights 1997, 2009

All rights reserved. No part of this book should be reproduced or transmitted in any form or by any means, electronic or mechanical, including photocopying, recording, or by any information storage and retrieval system without written permissions from the publisher.

Worldwide Publishing Group
7710-T Cherry Park Dr.
Houston, Texas 77095
1-800-569-4825
Web: http://www.EddieAndAlice.com
Resources: http://www.PrayerBookstore.com

You've been given a one-year scholarship to
Eddie and Alice's 52-week Online School of Prayer
http://www.TeachMeToPray.com

ISBN: 978-0-692-19456-0

How to use "spiritual mapping" to discern and defeat spiritual darkness in your city.

Contents

CHAPTER 1 - It's A Sin Issue..5

CHAPTER 2 - Root Bondage VS Prevailing Bondage 17

CHAPTER 3 - Discernment and Facts................................23

CHAPTER 4 - Prayer Journey to Goliad, Texas................31

CHAPTER 5 - Your City's Redemptive Gift......................41

CHAPTER 6 - Primary and Secondary Resources...........49

CHAPTER 7 - Prayer Journey to Riga, Latvia 57

CHAPTER 1
It's A Sin Issue

We can't win a city we don't love, and we can't love a city we hardly know. Love your city as you intercede for it. Love is the beginning of all freedom for us and our cities. It was God's love that initiated our freedom. It's important we learn about our cities if we expect to see them changed. As we discern the spiritual climate of our cities, we will pray more accurately, and believe God for change.

> In the early 70s, Eddie and I were invited to lead worship at a revival in a rural farming town in southern Oklahoma. I became sick that week and needed a doctor. When I entered the doctor's office, I was shocked to see the room filled with pregnant teenagers. *Something must be dreadfully wrong in this town*, I thought to myself.
>
> The next day, Eddie and I went to the local drugstore to buy personal items. As we entered the store, we noticed near

the front door a massive magazine rack, blatantly stocked with pornography. Around the rack were four or five junior high school boys scanning the nude pictures in the magazines. Much to the shock of the boys, Eddie walked over to the rack, collected all the pornographic material, took the magazines from the boys, and walked to the checkout counter.

The clerk asked what he wanted. He answered matter-of-factly, "Ma'am, I want to buy these pornographic magazines."

A bit astonished, seeing that the magazine stack was about 24-inches high, she asked in disbelief, "*All of them*?"

Eddie nodded, "yes."

She said, "Sir, I'm not sure I can sell all of them to you. Just a minute, please."

She went to ask the owner.

He too could hardly believe the request. So, they both returned.

The owner said, "Sir, what is it that you want?"

Eddie explained once again, "I want to buy all of these nasty magazines."

"All of them? Why?" The owner asked curiously.

Eddie said, "I am going to burn them."

The man angrily replied, "Sir, I don't sell magazines just to see them burned!"

With fire in his eyes, Eddie said sternly, "Sir, you are correct. That's *not* why you sell them. You sell these filthy magazines to pollute the minds of little boys like those over there (pointing to the boys) who had been reading them moments ago. Your town has a major problem with immorality and teenage pregnancy. You, sir, are contributing to the problem by selling this trash."

The man irritably reached to take the pile of magazines, and Eddie turned and said, "Sir, the Lord God just told me that if you don't remove this from your store, you will not live." And with that, we left.

The fear of God was palpable in the store. I could feel it and so could a few customers who were shopping at the time. Righteous indignation welled up as Eddie told the mocking man that God would hold him accountable for the lives of these young people.

Four weeks later we received a call from the pastor in Oklahoma. He told us that the drugstore owner was dead. He had eaten a peanut butter sandwich before bed and choked to death in his sleep. The pastor said, "A holy fear of God fell over our church the following Sunday, as many of my members repented and some gave their hearts to Jesus." Later the drugstore changed owners and the new owners removed all the pornography. Praise the Lord! All our cities need *this kind of change!*

Don't misunderstand! It is a tragedy that the man didn't repent. Eddie did not curse the man, he simply passed along God's warning. The man made his own choice. The Bible is very clear…*"It's not God's desire that any man should perish, but that all should come to repentance"* (2 Peter 3:9). The store owner refused the mercy that comes with repentance and salvation. God allowed Eddie and me to discern the spiritual climate of this small town. Remember the adage, "Some are too close to the forest to see the trees." Without spiritual discernment, it's hard to recognize the roots of darkness in your own city. Revelation is required.

Through this experience, the local church realized there were strongholds in their town they hadn't previously known. The good news is that it created a hunger in them to pray targeted, specific prayers for their community. *Specificity produces fervency.* It's the *"effectual, fervent prayer of a righteous person that avails much"* (James 5:16).

Our Strategy

1. Sin is the issue.
2. Prayer is the tool.
3. Partnership is the method.
4. Evangelism is the purpose.

Sin is the issue. The first step is to determine *what sin (or sins)* and the historical facts that opened the gates and established ungodly strongholds. This information allows people of prayer the opportunity to perform their priestly duty to go boldly into the presence of the Lord to repent for the sins of the original and previous inhabitants and ask for mercy on their behalf. This is the privilege of the Church, Christ's bride. However, if you feel compelled to address a demonic presence, be sure and get a confirmation in your heart from the Lord.

Identificational Repentance

Prayer and partnership are the methods. Included in this partnership is the concept of "identification repentance." Let's discuss this.

Jesus required moral responsibility of the Jews; nothing less should be expected of us. We have been given a biblical model and mandate to cancel these offenses through what we call identification repentance. It's the practice of repenting of sins and iniquities on behalf of our ancestors (or, in other situations, people groups, nations, cities, et al). Before you determine we are outside of biblical boundaries, just open your heart and mind to the

Scriptures. The accumulated influence of evil down through the generations is part of the defiled foundation we may have to deal with to experience complete freedom in our lives.

King David understood identification repentance: *"We have sinned with our fathers, we have committed iniquity, and we have done wickedly. Our fathers understood not thy wonders in Egypt; they remembered not the multitude of thy mercies"* (Ps. 106:6-7).

Jeremiah also engaged in identification repentance: *"We acknowledge, O Lord, our wickedness, and the iniquity of our fathers: for we have sinned against thee. Do not abhor us, for thy name's sake, do not disgrace the throne of thy glory: remember; break not thy covenant with us"* (Jer. 14:20-21, NKJV).

Nehemiah too understood the need for such repentance: *"Let thine ear now be attentive, and thine eyes open, that thou mayest hear the prayer of thy servant, which I pray before thee now, day and night, for the children of Israel, thy servants, and confess the sins of the children of Israel, which we have sinned against thee: both I and my father's house have sinned"* (Neh. 1:6, NKJV).

<u>Jesus too understood the need for such repentance</u>: *"Woe to you, teachers of the law and Pharisees, you hypocrites! You build tombs for the prophets and decorate the graves of the righteous. And you say, 'If we had lived in the days of our forefathers, we would not have taken part with them in shedding the blood of the prophets.' So you testify against yourselves that you are the descendants of those who murdered the prophets. Fill up, then, the measure of the sin of your forefathers."* Then a few verses later, Jesus says, *"And so upon you will come all the righteous blood that has been shed on earth, from the blood of righteous Abel to the blood of Zechariah son of Berekiah, whom you murdered between the temple and the altar. I tell you the truth; all this will come upon this generation"* (35-36).

Personal Responsibility for Sin

Some Christians refuse to believe that ancestral iniquity applies to us. They maintain that one's personal sin is all that is relevant. Some stake their claim on Ezekiel 18.

"What do you people mean by quoting this proverb about the land of Israel: 'The fathers eat sour grapes, and the children's teeth are set on edge?' As surely as I live, declares the Sovereign Lord, you will no longer quote this proverb in Israel" (vv. 2-3).

Ezekiel is referring to spiritual death as a consequence of sin. The point is that children won't suffer everlasting separation from God ("teeth to be set on edge") due to their fathers' sins; where a person spends eternity is his or her own choice. This passage clarifies it:

"Behold, all souls are mine; as the soul of the father, so also the soul of the son is mine: the soul that sinneth, it shall die.... The soul which does sin will be put to death: the son will not be made responsible for the evil-doing of the father, or the father for the evil-doing of the son" (verse 20).

That isn't about predisposition, it's about eternity. A person's decision to delight in sin and continue in it isn't a generational thing. It's an individual choice. Even if there is a generational iniquity operating in your family line, it isn't a license to perpetuate it... Break it!

The Hebrew fathers were responsible for teaching the laws of God to their children (Deut. 11:19) and not to do so carries a high price (Deut. 11:26-28). This is as true for us as it was for them. But the way it's true is different. As we see in Jeremiah 31:31-34:

> *"Behold, the days come, saith Jehovah, that I will make a new covenant with the house of Israel, and with the house of Judah: not according to the covenant that I made with*

their fathers in the day that I took them by the hand to bring them out of the land of Egypt; which my covenant they brake, although I was a husband unto them, saith Jehovah. But this is the covenant that I will make with the house of Israel after those days, saith Jehovah: I will put my law in their inward parts, and in their heart will I write it; and I will be their God, and they shall be my people: and they shall teach no more every man his neighbor, and every man his brother, saying, Know Jehovah; for they shall all know me, from the least of them unto the greatest of them, saith Jehovah: for I will forgive their iniquity, and their sin will I remember no more."

In the study of the Bible, we must discern truth considering the whole, not just one portion. Jeremiah isn't contradicting himself. He's not saying that people can't suffer for the sins of their fathers; rather, he's saying that anyone who experiences eternal death will do so because of his own sin, not anyone else's (verse 30). In the next chapter Jeremiah says of God, *"You have mercy on thousands, and send punishment*

> *for the evil-doing of the fathers on their children after them"* (32:18). [1]

Our ultimate reason to engage in spiritual mapping is to discern the truth about our cities so we can conduct warfare prayer. What is the purpose? We do this to provoke a shift in the spiritual atmosphere of our cities, so unhindered evangelism can occur that will extend the kingdom of God. Every Christian is aware that sin is our ultimate problem. Romans 3:23 says, *"For all have sinned, and come short of the glory of God."* Sin separates us from God and sins hold cities in bondage as well. Sodom, Gomorrah, and Nineveh were both identified with their sins. Sins perpetuated by the residents allowed unclean spirits to mark and establish a territorial presence in those cities.

The same is true today. The mere mention of some cities suggests the names of their ruling spirits. For instance: When we think of San Francisco, California, we think of "homosexuality." When we consider Moscow, Russia, we think of the "anti-Christ spirit." Rome, Italy suggests a "religious spirit." Bangkok, Thailand we consider "spirit of whoredom." We think Tokyo, Japan or New York City, "Pride" comes to mind. Salem, Massachusetts? "Witchcraft" is our first thought because of the witch trials during the 1600s.

CHAPTER 2
Root Bondage VS Prevailing Bondage

Sin is any deviation from the will of God. If the initial sin is not repented of, it opens a door to darkness. In time, if the root sin is revisited, it's reinforced. The root sin revisited will not only grow--it will morph into different expressions. These expressions of the root bondage we call "the prevailing bondage."

Ezekiel 22:30 says that God is looking for someone *who will stand in the gap for the land!* Did you get that? Stand in the gap 'for the land.' Ancient moguls and kings, as well as dictators, knew that if you can capture the land, you can control the residents. Here are some key considerations:

- <u>Root bondage</u> goes back to the *original sin against the land.*
- <u>Prevailing bondage</u> is nothing but the *systematic recurrence over time* of a deeper bondage and other expressions of related sin.
- The <u>root bondage</u> may or may not relate to the present day <u>prevailing bondage</u> because *sin changes as people change*!
- However, if we are going to strike a significant blow to the plans of the enemy, it's crucial we learn the source of the root bondage,

established by the original (often the native) people of the area. The reality is historical facts don't change. Facts are truths firmly set in time.

In the United States, for example, the Native Americans were the original landowners. Some were animists who believed that natural elements such as mountains, rivers, trees, thunder, fire, stars, animals, and humans are linked to a pervasive and conscious spiritual life force. Many Native Americans sought the intervention of "rain gods," "sun gods" and "harvest gods." Instead of keeping covenant with the living God, many original inhabitants of made pacts with demons in return for rain or a good harvest.

How has the deception adapted or mutated into the current culture of our cities? We can identify the spiritual continuum as it relates to behavior in society. Like where there are concentrated pockets of homosexuality, or areas in the city that are gospel resistant, the original root bondage has adapted to the 21st Century. Consider areas of your city plagued with excessive death, poverty, perversion, greed or witchcraft.

Another instance is the original pacts men made with Satan have adapted to expressions we see in present society. For instance, Texas' Karankawan Indians were known to practice homosexuality. The fact that we have a large community of homosexuals in one section of Houston is no coincidence. The sexual perversion practiced by the Karankawans in the 1500's is well-documented. So, it's easy to track the original root bondage to the prevailing bondage we see in Houston today. Many intercessory prayer groups have gone to strategic historical sites in Houston to pray and repent for the early lack of stewardship of our land. Our results have encouraged Christians citywide because the nation's largest churches are in Houston. Best of all, what once was a militant homosexual community in our city has been more open to the gospel in recent years. Have we experienced complete success? No, but I believe we are moving in the right direction.

Suppose, as we research the history of a town, we learn that there was a massacre in the 1600's in the same area where a high death rate now exists. If we know this piece of history, we can see why there is so much death in that specific part of town. Habakkuk 2:8 says, *"Because you have plundered many nations, the peoples who are left will plunder you. <u>For you have shed man's blood</u>; you have destroyed lands and cities and everyone in them."* Shedding innocent blood defiles the land. (Numbers 25:33)

Cities with the Highest Homicide Rates

It may surprise you to know that the highest homicidal crime (per capita) city in the U.S. in 2018 is St. Louis, Missouri. This notorious "badge of death" doesn't happen out of nothing. The ancient Cahokia Mounds state historical site (circa 1050-1350 CE) is the site of a pre-Columbian North American city at the Mississippi River at modern-day St. Louis, Missouri.

The Cahokia Mounds is the largest and most complex archeological site north of the pre-Columbian cities in Mexico. To get an idea of its size, in 1988, the mound was calculated to be roughly the same size at its base as the Great Pyramid of Giza in Egypt. The major difference between two is that the Pyramid of Giza is made entirely from stone, but the Cahokia Mound (which is one of 80) is almost entirely constructed from baskets filled with soil and clay.

Excavations through the years have uncovered mass-graves and bones. The original root of death uncovered by archeology continues to flow down into the lives of St. Louis' present-day residents.

To see how the St. Louis crime-rate compares to other major U.S. cities, go to https://bit.ly/2nuCU6Q

Habakkuk 2:12 declares, *"Woe to him who <u>builds a city with bloodshed</u> and <u>establishes a town by crime</u>!"* Shedding innocent blood is one of the numerous ways our land can be defiled. And obviously, defilement opens doors to demonic contracts. Other ways the land can be defiled is through prostitution, adultery, breaking covenants, changing the laws of God into the laws of man, bloodshed, idolatry, and possibly other ways I haven't yet discovered in the Scripture.

It's not an accident on the part of Satan to ignite school shootings, police murders, or mass killings in churches. The devil wants to mark his territory and establish a town by bloodshed. Jeremiah understood this. He was telling the children of Israel to turn from their wickedness. Instead, the priests and the prophets threatened his life. His response? *"Be assured, however, that if you put me to death, you will bring the guilt of innocent blood on yourselves and on this city and on those who live in it, for in truth the Lord has sent me to you to speak all these words in your hearing"* (Jer. 26:15).

CHAPTER 3
Discernment and Facts

If we are to pray effectively for our cities, we must have *discernment*. I am reminded of an old joke about a church that was about to vote on the purchase of a new chandelier for their auditorium.

An elderly gentleman stood to address the congregation. "I'm against the purchase of a new chandelier for three reasons," he explained. "First, I can't spell chandelier. Second, no one in our church knows how to play one. And third, what we really need in this sanctuary is more light!" Obviously, the man *did not* have discernment. ☺

How can we utilize spiritual discernment? We can mobilize a team who will pray through the research we've compiled and seek God for a strategy. Proverbs 24:6, *"If you go to war, you need guidance. If you want to win, you need many good advisers."*

Consider these guidelines:

    1. The strategy must be scriptural. (Proverbs 19:2)
    2. The team should realize the power of their unity, and guard it in prayer. (Psalms 139)

3. The team should divide the city or town into manageable smaller sections that they can research. Don't try to tackle too many projects at a time. (Ezekiel 4)

4. With this new research information, ask God to confirm your assumptions. (Acts 5:32)

5. Research, study, prepare and discern, but *never* go to war without a clear word from the Holy Spirit. Another scripture that emphasizes good advice is, *"Make plans by asking for guidance. If you go to war, get good advice"* (Proverbs 20:18).

6. Don't rush. To spiritually map an area properly will take considerable time.

Diagnosis doesn't always mean assignment.

Just because you have identified and diagnosed a demonic root in your city doesn't mean you have permission from the Lord to conduct warfare. The diagnosis is only one step; there are many others to follow. Ask the Holy Spirit to confirm that you are on track. 2 Corinthians 13:1 says, *"Every matter must be established by the testimony of two or three witnesses."* Establish an accountability system with pastors, prayer leaders, elders or anyone who knows Scripture and is a balanced godly person. After all, the team needs to utilize diverse spiritual gifts to maintain balance and continuity.

Guard yourself and your team against adopting a limited vision. For example: Your city may have a high divorce rate or large pockets of gangs, so you assume these are the root problems. Never determine a belief about an entire city based on a single issue. What is true for one part of a town may not be true for another. Make no mistake; spiritual mapping is an extensive research project that when done well, could take years.

Fortunately, God has intercessors that will pay the price for both short and long-term assignments. One of the things I love about spiritual strategizing is that you can do the work little by little. By the way, search out others in your city who have already invested many hours, days, and years researching your city. I assure you there are those who have already done much of the work. Now you are the next in the relay race to pick up the baton and run with it.

If we are to discern properly, it's crucial we relate rightly to God and with one another. We can't pray "Thy kingdom come" until we will say "my kingdom go." For instance, if we pray and repent for racial prejudice in our city, yet have an unresolved division in our hearts, we won't be effective. First, reconcile your relationships, then return to the warfare and mapping. James says it well, *"To him, that knows to do good, and does it not, to him it is sin"* (James 4:17). This is why it's important to have a teachable and transparent team. In spiritual warfare, the devil and his demons do not play fair. They intend to "divide and conquer." Grievances, unforgiveness, hidden sins and personal strongholds disqualify a person from proper discernment and will impact the entire team. (1 John 1:9)

Another requirement, if we're to discern the spiritual climate of our city, is to have a growing level of intimacy with the Father. Scripture says, *"The Lord confides in those who fear him, and he reveals his secrets to them"* (Psalms 25:14). God is looking for people who will develop an intimate relationship with Him. This requires an investment of time in private prayer. One's desire for intimacy depends upon the condition of his or her heart. Proverbs 23:7 says, *"As a man thinks in his heart so is he."* As our heart is, so are we before the Lord. We can advance no further into the holy place of the Father's presence than our heart is prepared by the Holy Spirit to go. Our heart and mind must be committed to spiritual intimacy with God.

Our minds gather knowledge from God's Word. Our

understanding of the Word deals with intellectual ideas and mental images of divine things. But those can't reach the real life of the inner spirit. It's in our spirit (heart) that God dwells by His Holy Spirit. He is there for us to build a bridge to God's presence and provide power for intimacy. Our willingness to grow in intimacy with God will help our spiritual discernment. And remember this: *you will have limited authority over demonic principalities if you have limited spiritual intimacy with God.*

Finally, it's necessary to have a personal commitment to your city. I've heard people criticize their city, the traffic, the climate, or any number of other attributes. They'll say something like, "I can't wait to retire and get out of this town." Why would the Lord choose to reveal to you the vital insights about your city if you don't love your city, but instead you are looking for the first opportunity to leave it?

In Jeremiah 29, God had the prophet send a letter to the Israelites who were being held captive in Babylon. He exhorted them to...

1. *"Build houses and settle down"* (verse 5)
2. *"Plant gardens and eat what is produced"* (verse 5)
3. *"Marry and have children"* (verse 6)

While living in the evil empire of Babylon, God told His people to seek the peace and prosperity of the city, and pray to the Lord for it, because if it prospered, so would they. (verse 7) The Lord backed up His promise in verses 11-14, *"For I know the plans I have for you, declares the Lord, plans to prosper you and not to harm you, plans to give you hope and a future."* Then in verse fourteen, he reveals his purpose. *"I will bring you back from captivity; I will gather you from all nations..."*

What was the Father saying? The message then was, as it is today: "bloom where you are planted!" We are to plant seeds in prayer, water the soil with our tears, and watch faithfully until harvest time. Now fall in love with your city. If you must leave one city for another, fall in love with the new one. Let's consider some important keys to effectively research.

1. Objective Facts

To be effective, stay biblical, practical, and credible. The strongest tools in spiritual mapping are *objective facts!* A revelation or vision is only as effective as the objective fact that backs it up. Objective information is historical, documented evidence that explains the reasons certain spiritual darkness is present. As my friend, researcher and author George Otis Jr. says, "Facts kick." We can't change history. Our job is to uncover historical facts that can help us redeem the future.

2. Subjective Impressions

Other helpful tools are *subjective impressions*. Subjective impressions come from visions, dreams, words of knowledge and prophecy. At best, the Apostle Paul teaches, *"For now we see through a glass darkly,"* and *"... we know in part and we prophesy in part"* (1 Cor. 13:9, 12). So, we should never draw conclusions from our *subjective impressions* alone.

Impressions and discernment work together. It's true; discernment is a walk in the light, not a leap in the dark. Effective warfare won't be accomplished with subjective impressions alone. There should be corroborating confirming evidence. (Read Matthew 18:16; 2 Corinthians 13:1; 1 Timothy 5:19; and Hebrews 10:28.) So, the two tools of the age of spiritual city reaching are <u>objective facts</u> and <u>subjective impressions,</u> which work together to deliver a clear picture as to how to pray.

CHAPTER 4
Prayer Journey to Goliad, Texas

One of my team's spiritual warfare trips was to pray for Goliad, Texas; which is not too far from San Antonio. My prayer team had previous warfare experience on prayer journeys, so we were able to flow together in the strength of our individual spiritual gifts. The Texas Gulf Coast area around Goliad has a rich history, of which the native Karankawan Indians were part.

Contrary to the impression Hollywood movies may have left us with, most Native American tribes were and are peace-loving, gentle groups. But the Karankawans were different. They were a vicious, murderous tribe.

I had taken a few intercessors to the research library in downtown Houston. Once there, we sat down in a quiet room to read. We were shocked to read in book after book things like,

> "They are cruel, inhuman and ferocious. When one nation makes war with another, the one that conquers puts all

the old men and old women to the knife and carries off the little children for food to eat on the way; the other children are sold; the vagabonds and grown women and young girls are carried off to serve them, with the exception of some whom they reserve to sacrifice in the dance before their gods and saints." [2]

In the historical book *Spain's New Territory* we find:

"Karankawans inhabited this land back to the time when the memory of man runneth not to the contrary; they were the original settlers and all others were intruders. Research has not yet established the age of the tribe of these Indians. One scholar believes they are related to a tribe of giants found on the coast of California, but the reference is rather vague. Another writer relates them to a group of aborigines who inhabited the Texas Big Bend thousands of years ago, and he goes on to tie them in with the Abilene man, the oldest known type of human to reside in Texas. Linguistically, the Karankawa belong generally to the Coahiltecan family found to the southwest of them." [3]

In the year 1528, the Spaniards began to arrive in the new world, usually in three waves: as explorers, conquistadors, and missionaries.

James Day, the writer of *The Gulf Coast Cannibals* wrote,

> "The explorer Cabeza de Vaca, along with eighty Spaniards ran aground on the island of Malhado along the Texas Gulf Coast, in the land of the Karankawa. Cabeza de Vaca had many struggles with the Indians, and after a short time left them to their own territory. The Karankawa Indians were left alone for a century and a half while the French and Spaniards fought and argued for the control of the Gulf of Mexico. Cabeza de Vaca and his companions were no doubt forgotten by the Karankawa by the time the Frenchman, Rene' Robert Caveliar, Sieur de la Salle, appeared among them." [4]

In the summer of 1684, LaSalle left France with a

contingent of 400 men. Their intention was to control the New World, which included the Karankawa territory. Having missed a turn in their ocean voyage, they landed in Matagorda Bay on Texas' Gulf Coast. Author Mr. Day writes,

> "Between February and July 1685, La Salle moved his headquarters around the Gulf Coast area and finally settled among the native Indians. Using timbers from the wrecked ship, Amiable, La Salle dubbed the place Fort St. Louis in honor of his king." [5]

Their hard work and determination in the South Texas heat eventually produced a fort worthy of notice for the French explorers and their families. Note: The purpose of giving you this background is to illustrate how one intercessor's revelation became the necessary "puzzle piece" that was required for us to complete our prayer assignment using *objective facts* and *subjective impressions*.

For three years the Frenchmen and Karankawan Indians continually clashed over territorial rights.

> "Then, on Christmas Eve, 1688, as the French were preparing for festivities on

the morrow, their Karankawa neighbors appeared for a little celebration of their own. They had word that the great French leader, La Salle, was dead, and they declared their belief that all Frenchmen should die with their leaders. Inside the fort, the Indians began their attack, and they killed every white man and woman there except those who broke and ran. Escape was not possible as the running French were pursued and promptly dispatched. Only four or five children were spared as Fort St. Louis came to a dramatic, predictable end.

When two Frenchmen returned, they discovered the mess. Everything was destroyed, and fourteen bodies were discovered and buried. The houses were all sacked, the furniture was broken, and over two hundred books in French had been torn apart and the pages scattered. Outside were three dead bodies that had been overlooked." [6]

This incident is one of the earliest recorded premeditated bloodsheds between the white man and Native Americans on Texas' Gulf Coast.

For our prayer team, this was important. We had three journals that documented the evidence. However, we had a serious problem. Fort St. Louis no longer exists. Our prayer team would require divine guidance if we were to pray (as we say), "on-site with insight." Before we left Houston on our prayer journey, one of my intercessors came to me with a dream she had. In her dream, she felt she heard the Lord say, "*Natural gas pipeline explosion in the Goliad area. Tell Alice.*"

When she awoke, the Lord gave her the Scripture: Ezekiel 12:16. "*But I will <u>spare a few of them from the sword</u>, famine, and plague, so that in the nations where they go they may acknowledge all their detestable practices. Then they will know that I am the Lord.*"

Why only "a few" spared? This Scripture was confirmation of the events that happened at Fort St. Louis hundreds of years ago. In fact, it was the survivors who reported what happened the night of that dreadful bloodshed in 1688.

Now more than 300 years later, God spoke to an intercessory prayer group to research the history (where the history books said Fort St. Louis was) and

receive the burden to pray and repent for the shedding of innocent blood on the land.
(Read Ezekiel 22:2-4; Hosea 4:2-3; Ezekiel 7:23, 9:9; Isaiah 5:7; 1 Samuel 25: 31; Numbers 35: 33-34; Deuteronomy 17: 8; and Deuteronomy 19:10.)

Once we arrived near Garcitas Creek, where our research indicated the fort had once stood), we decided to ask around to see if anyone in the area knew where the original Fort St. Louis might have been located along the creek. Remarkably, an old ranch hand, working the land of the French survivor's descendants, told us: "They say the fort was just above the natural gas line that protrudes from the bank of the creek."

What! We could hardly believe our ears! Approaching the creek on foot, sure enough, across the creek from where we stood, coming out of the water was a large natural gas pipeline with the words: *Warning: Natural Gas Pipeline.* Immediately my intercessor's word rang true. We were looking at the place where the original fort had stood so many years before, the site of the great bloodbath. We were standing on the opposite bank, which was as close as we could get.

An intense burden fell on each of us. At first, we

could barely form the words to pray. It was so surreal how the revelation and reality were coming together. It was as if it had been our loved ones who had suffered such cruelty so many years earlier. Then we sensed the anointing to repent for the offenses of the French, and the wickedness of the Karankawans. We asked God to cleanse the land from the defilement. As we walked away knowing we had obeyed the Lord, a supernatural cool breeze blew in our faces, even though we were in the middle of a hot, humid, July, Texas summer. I believe this was God's confirmation that He was pleased with our perseverance. The facts kicked—we had the *objective evidence*; the research proved true! Yet, the *subjective revelation* from the dream was the missing piece of the puzzle. This we call "a word of knowledge." (1 Cor. 12:8) It was something of which we had no natural knowledge. When we combined the research with our revelation, God used us as a strategic assault team to weaken the foundation of darkness.

We always look for confirmation that we have hit a target. The first confirmation was the cool breeze that mysteriously began to blow.

Our second confirmation came about an hour later as we were eating lunch in town. A woman, recognizing that we weren't from Goliad, approached our table.

She said she was the manager of the Goliad Historical Museum, where lots of Texas history is kept. She asked why we were in town. I responded, "Do you really want to know?"

Somewhat surprised by my question, she replied, "Yes."

I explained to her that we were praying Christians from Houston to whom God had given a burden for her town. Tears welled up in her eyes. She explained that just the day before, she was in a ladies Bible study/prayer meeting where someone in the group mentioned the need for prayer help for Goliad. They briefly prayed for God to answer their prayer! ... Well, God DID answer their prayer. And, we were blessed to be part of the answer!

As we saw during our journey to Goliad, the strongholds are established through sin. Once the original sin is identified, and historical evidence validates it, prayer is the tool that will change the spiritual environment. Where facts kick, prayer conquers!

CHAPTER 5
Your City's Redemptive Gift

Another consideration we should have when trying to discern the spiritual climate of a city is to ask the Lord what its *redemptive gift* might be. A redemptive gift can be defined as a distinct characteristic of that city that God can use to demonstrate His divine truth and blessing. What is true about a city in the natural will often be true in the Spirit.

For instance, the first name given to Jerusalem was *Salem*. (Genesis 14:18-20) *Salem* means "peace." *Jerusalem* means "habitation of peace." God's redemptive plan is to see Jerusalem be a habitation of peace for all nations. Is it now? No. Will it be? Yes! In fact, all of Psalm 122 is dedicated to praying the truth about the City of Jerusalem. Until Jerusalem is a city of peace, Satan will focus on replacing the redemptive gift of Jerusalem (peace) with a destructive gift. The reason? He will do so to prevent the city from ever reaching its God-ordained prophetic purpose.

How do you decide what might be the redemptive gift for your city? Let's consider some. What are the most outstanding features of your city?

- Hospitals?
- Technology?
- Waterways?
- Trade?
- Entertainment?
- Its residents?
- Manufacturing?
- Agriculture?
- Historical Landmarks?
- Mountains?
- Climate?
- Tourism?

Example:

Houston, Texas, where I live, is known for its advanced Medical centers. We have some of the most-acclaimed Cancer treatment hospitals anywhere in the world. Houston is also known for oil. We have huge underground storage facilities with more than 100 million barrels of crude oil. We have a network of large oil pipelines. We have seagoing oil tankers docking in Houston, and many refineries surround the city. Because of the medical hospitals, crude, and refined oil, many prophetic voices believe Houston's redemptive gift is to be a healer for the nations. Through our words, our prayers, our love, our unity, our serving the sick, we Christians can offer spiritual healing to the nations as well.

It was no accident that more than 100,000 people from New Orleans were bused or flown to Houston following Hurricane Katrina in 2005. The Astrodome was set as a triage center and thousands of Houstonians answered the call to serve those displaced people. Food, clothes, money, medical aid, and lodging were provided. What CNN, ABC, NBC, Fox News, CBS or MSNBC didn't report were the huge numbers of Christians who prayed for and led many of them to Christ during the crisis. The devil will always work counter to your city's redemptive gift by dashing your hopes that lives can be changed, or by suppressing the work of the Holy Spirit in the local churches or ministries. However, if we stay attentive to God's assignments it is possible to see restorative work.

On August 25th, 2017, Hurricane Harvey, a Category 4 storm hit Texas. According to the National Hurricane Center, it caused $125 billion dollars in damage. That's more than any other natural disaster in U.S history except Hurricane Katrina. Texas Governor Greg Abbott needed more than $125 billion in federal relief. It affected 13-million people from Texas through Louisiana, Mississippi, Tennessee, and Kentucky. As of October 13, 2017, at least 88 people had died from the storm.

Harvey made landfall three times in six days. At its peak on September 1, 2017, one-third of Houston was underwater. Two feet of rain fell in the first 24 hours. Flooding forced 39,000 people out of their homes and into shelters. Dallas created a mega-shelter for 5,000 evacuees out of its main convention center.

As of September 5, 2017, Hurricane Harvey had damaged over 325,000 homes, of which 12,700 were destroyed. Federal forces rescued 10,000 people who were trapped in their homes or on flooded highways.

Yet, this was our opportunity to display to the world,

a city that helps its own. News agencies far and wide marveled at the community action for fellow Houstonians. What was a grave disaster, God used for our good! Neighborhoods helped one another. Many Houstonians (and those all over the **nations lent a hand** to total strangers who needed help.

Eddie and I were assisting friends with removing water-soaked drywall and ruined furniture. And it was amazing how women and men came from all over the nation to rescue people and animals in our area. The national news broadcast Houston as the city that cares, and we became an example of how to manage a storm. It was a redemptive time for the

Greater Houston area and pulled our community together. Do we want to go through that again? *No!* ☺

We have been discussing the gifts of your city, but what about the churches in your city? What about the redemptive gifts of its churches?

There are unique churches in every city. What does the church you attend have that other churches in the area not have? Is your church exceptionally structured for missions? Do you know some churches that have powerful prayer ministries? What about churches that are great at evangelism? How about equipping churches that excel in their teaching and training methods?

Instead of becoming critical and divided, let's celebrate and thank God for the contribution each church brings to our cities. Each church plays a unique part in extending God's kingdom in your city.

Just as we individually have spiritual gifts, i.e. prophecy, teaching, administration, discerning of spirits, our churches often operate in the spiritual gifts on which they were originally founded.

Discern the potential for spiritual breakthrough by asking:

1. Is there the beginning of unity among Pastors from various denominations?
2. Can you see the beginning of cultural or gender unity?
3. Are there regular city prayer meetings?
4. Do you see active reconciliation between Christian leaders and laypeople?
5. Are there intercessory prayer groups that meet faithfully?
6. Are there indications that God has begun to answer prayer (such as reduced crime, public apologies, cooperation among denominations, etc.?)

Next, find out who named your city? Learn the meaning of its name. Was your city named after a person? If so, was that person godly or ungodly? Was your city established on a wicked foundation, such as fraud, lies, bloodshed, or broken contracts? Regardless, keep in mind that all sin opens doors to the enemy and those doors need to be closed. If you discover that your city was built on an unholy foundation, you can be the one to pray for change.

CHAPTER 6
Primary and Secondary Resources

Commit to fast and pray for the Lord to reveal both the redemptive and destructive aspects of your city. The Lord can't lay claim on our cities until He first lays claim on us.

1. Primary Resources

Remember, the primary method of discerning the spiritual strongholds in a city is through historical research. The concept of spiritual mapping is to discover evidence (facts) that the prayer team can bring in intercession before the Father. The research team is like a team of "spiritual detectives and surveyors" skilled at sorting through information. The researchers look for documented ways the devil has developed demonic pacts to keep people in deception. The group must learn to differentiate between superfluous information and the serious spiritual trigger points. Beware of chasing rabbits. Remain focused and purpose-centered. Primary sources, like old original maps or surveys, revered waterways or springs, mounds, important roads, nature spots, known battlefields or massacre sights which need no interpretation, prove to be the best to research.

Recently, we were in Bucharest, Romania to teach pastors from Romania and Maldives. Our host is a godly businessman whose business is to build and repair trains throughout Romania. While we were there, Stefan, our host asked Eddie and me to pray for his staff and his office buildings. When we arrived at the business, it was clear that the buildings had been there for 50+ years. The deep red brick buildings had a history of oppression. It was a sobering time for us.

During WWII, Romania was involved in what was called "The Pogrom," which was the systematic antisemitic incarceration and massacre of thousands of Jews. Their neighbors, the police, and the army rounded up entire Jewish families. Some were stabbed, many were beaten to death with crowbars, and some shot to death. Others were loaded onto trains to be carted off to concentration camps. History records one train was crammed with 5,000 Jews. Only 1,011 actually survived the seven-day trip. Romanian police found 1,258 bodies, and hundreds of bodies were thrown from the train in transit. We felt our being there was significant.

Pushing aside the thought of men and women who had suffered during the war, we made our way toward the offices. Eddie and I prayed for Stefan's managers, lawyers, surveyors, clerks, and payroll staff. Each of them seemed grateful for our prayers. The entire time, however, I kept seeing in a brief vision the building that was parallel to the one we were in. I asked the owner if we could go outside and to the other building, of which he fully agreed.

When we walked outside, the dark presence of the building across from us was strong. The closer we got, the stronger it was to sense. The owner and property foreman said they had never entered this section of the building even though Stefan had owned it since 1991. There was a door and to the right of the door was a small window with oversized vertical bars set in concrete. The four of us moved toward the door, and as we did the cold wind swept between the two buildings where we were walking. With a little hesitation, the property manager pulled until the heavy steel door gave way and opened.

Even after so many decades, the demonic presence of suffering and death lingered. Inside the room and to the right was a vast deep, dark hole in the rubble-filled floor. None of us dared venture very close. The eerie spiritual awareness that possibly many men's, women's, and children's bones lay at the bottom of that dark pit was enough for us to halt and pray on the spot. We did just that! I can't say after praying that everything seemed to shift to a clean and bright atmosphere. There had been so much violation, one fifteen-minute prayer wasn't enough. But Eddie and I had carried out the assignment given us. Some violations are so grievous to the heart of God, that more prayer and research are necessary to complete the job.

2. Secondary Resources

The next information to glean is from secondary resources. These are interpreted sources of history like articles, insurance records, spiritual quest sites, occult temples, police reports, diaries, broadcasts, journals, newspapers, books, college dissertations, historical libraries and personal interviews.

Other important items to look for are monuments, icons, markers that honor men, or obelisks. The Old Testament calls obelisks "high places" or "Asherah poles." The Hebrew word *Asherah* means "pillar or image of wood." It was set up with the image of Baal and worshipped by sexual rites of perverse practices. Asherah comes from the root word, *Ashar*, to be straight, upright, and erect. The pillar was set upright or erect in the ground like a totem pole. The people sometimes would cut off the top of a living tree in the form of a pyramid or phallic (male sex organ at erection). Some Scriptures speak of the Asherah as a "grove" describing groups of trees. (Read Exodus 34:13; Deuteronomy 7:5; 12:3; 16:21; Judges 3:7; Isaiah 17:8; 27:9; Jeremiah 17:2; and Micah 5:14.)

Originally the Asherah idol was worshipped as a symbol of the tree of life. Then later, it was perverted to mean the "origin of life," and pictured with the male organs of procreation (Ezekiel 16:17). These symbols became objects of worship and were accompanied by various forms of impurity. The perversion by devotees included demonic sexual orgies. The worship, which centered on the Canaanite nations, spread to other nations. Relics have been found, specifically among these heathen groups. The first mention of the Asherah idol in the Bible distinctly reveals God's hatred, and it was concerning this Asherah idol that He revealed Himself as "a Jealous God." (Read Exodus 34:13-14; 1 Kings 14:15; 15:13; 16:32-33; and 2 Chronicles 36:14.) This wicked behavior led to the destruction of the Canaanite nations and caused a lot of agony for Israel.

Another form of the Asherah was the fertility goddess, Ashtaroth. The Israelites experienced God's rejection when *"they forsook Him and served Baal and Ashtaroth"* (Judges 2:13). (For more study on the Asherah and Ashtareth read 1 Kings 11:5-6, 33; 14:11-12, 22-24; 16:30-33; 2 Kings 14:4, 17:9-12, 16-17; 18:4; 23:8-14; and Jeremiah 5:7-9.)

What do we learn from these sources? We learn that Satan is like a dog, who marks his territory with every sort of defilement. God has said, *"The earth is the Lord's and everything in it, the world, and all who live in it"* (Psalm 24:1). The devil and his minions are in the business of taking what belongs to God and extending his evil borders. For instance, *"God declares this is what the LORD says: For three sins of Ammon, even for four, I will not turn back my wrath, because he ripped open the pregnant women of Gilead to extend his borders"* (Amos 1:13).

It's time we learn who we are in Christ—dominion takers! Genesis 1:28 states, *"God blessed them (Adam and Eve) and said to them, 'Be fruitful and increase in number; fill the earth and subdue it and have dominion over...'"* The Hebrew word for subduing means to "tread down, conquer and bring into subjection." The word for dominion means to "tread down with the foot as an authority." Dominion is a word of royalty, kingship, and rulership. As priests unto God, we have been given dominion authority. (2 Peter 1:9; Revelations 1:6, 9) I love *The Message* version that says; *"The heaven of heavens is for God, but he put us in charge of the earth"* (Psalm 115:16, emphasis mine). So, let's *take charge*, okay? We are, to a large degree, responsible for what happens here on earth.

CHAPTER 7
Prayer Journey to Riga, Latvia

I looked forward to our prayer journey to Latvia. The Republic of Latvia, a Baltic nation in northern Europe, was part of the old Soviet Union. Eddie and I, along with a team of intercessors from our church, went to minister in Latvia's prisons, schools, and churches. However, I didn't know that a great spiritual warfare breakthrough awaited us.

I had never studied Latvia's history until I had a dream five-months before we departed. Let's be honest, friend. Some dreams come from the Lord, some from demons, some from our psyche, and even some *come from the previous night's spicy food we ate.* Discernment is often required to tell the difference. After prayer, other intercessors, including Eddie, felt this dream was from God.

In the dream, I was standing with a team of people at a city square facing a town filled with old buildings. With my right hand pointing at a 45-degree angle toward the Baltic Sea, I said, "One power point (spots that connect spiritual ley-lines) is an old fortress along the edge of the water."* Then I said, "Another key power point is where we are now standing."

Then I looked to the left and said, "I don't know what the power point is to the left of here." I woke up amazed but bewildered at such a strange dream. After recording the dream, I shared it with Eddie. There were three strategic lines and points in my dream that needed to be understood. I began to research what this could mean. This is a little of what I learned.

> * British Alfred Watkins, who published his classic work *The Old Straight Track* in 1925, coined the term *ley-line*. On a high hilltop, Watkins noticed that prehistoric sites on the Map fell into straight alignment. These can include ancient burial mounds, stone circles, churches (it was the policy of the early Catholic Church to reuse pagan sites by building their churches on traditional holy sites of the pagan past), hilltops, crossroads, river fords, holy wells, city gates, massacre sites, and obelisks. These sites (points) are where ley-lines intersect. [7]

George Otis, Jr. defines ley-lines as "geographic continuums of spiritual power that are established – or at least recognized – by the early inhabitants of an area. They may be viewed as conduits through which spiritual authority flows." [8] The concept of spiritual power points connected by ley-lines is a controversial issue. However, if the severing of ley-lines produces a positive spiritual result evidenced in the social structure of a society, then your discernment was correct.

Ley-lines and boundaries are similar in concept. Boundaries are spoken of 59 times in the Bible. I encourage you to read these verses and conduct a word search on your own. (Read Numbers 34:3-12, Deuteronomy 19:14, 27:17; Joshua 22:25; Job 24:2, 26:10; Psalms 6:6, 104:9; Proverbs 8:29, 22:28, 23:10; Jeremiah 5:22; Ezekiel 47:15-20; Hosea 5:10; and 2 Corinthians 10:15-16.)

Arriving in the fall in Latvia, I thought I was going to freeze to death! It was November and to the Latvians the weather was mild. To me, it felt icy! I have never been so cold in my life. As we drove through the city, to my surprise, I noticed the City Square I had seen in my dream. I asked our translator Maija about it.

She replied, "Oh that is where Lenin's statue sat until we lassoed it and pulled it down in 1991. Do you remember seeing us dismantle it on CNN, she asked?"

In fact, I did remember watching it on CNN. Fully convinced that my dream was from God, I told the team what we were to do. Eddie asked me if I could recall where each of us was standing in my dream. Amazingly, I did.

He said, "Then why don't you put each of us in the same position here as you saw us five months ago in your dream?" As I did, I realized that the dream I had had was months before some of the team *had even decided to go*. Now, here we were!

After I experienced the dream, I researched some of Latvia's history. The tourist guide of Old Riga said,

> "Nearly four thousand years before, the earliest Baltic people first occupied and settled on the Eastern Shore of the Baltic Sea. Livs, Letts, Lithuanians and Russian traders and craftspeople mainly inhabited this settlement. They built ships, forged weapons, carved amber, wood, and bone." [9]

The book continued,

> "They worshipped pagan gods' Perkons (Thunder), Saule (Sun), Laima, Dekla, and others." [10]

From 800-1150 A.D. the Vikings raided them from the west while the Russians plundered them from the east. This led to the formation of 320 sites of fortified castles in Latvian territory. One hundred and sixty were placed along the eastern border as a barrier to the insatiable expansion of the Russian Empire. Fear and death controlled the Latvians all but 40 precious years of independence. Then on August 21, 1991, Latvia's parliament declared their full independence from the Soviet Union.

Now back to my story. Two days later we stood on the spot where Lenin's statue had once stood. Our feet were freezing. I began to play out my dream, as I had seen it months before. As I mentioned, Eddie had me position each person according to the places they were standing in my dream.

When I pointed to my right, Maija said, "Where you are pointing is the Old Riga Castle, which was built in 1330." It had served as a watchtower during the wars, a residence for Polish and Swedish rulers, barracks for soldiers, and later the Russian Governor's headquarters. Up to the 17th Century, the castle was surrounded by a moat. (A moat is a deep and wide water-filled security trench around a castle.) The castle was known as a place where fear, control, and deception had ruled.

Understanding a little of the history, we spoke aloud to the fear and control that had gripped the Latvian people for centuries. With one voice we canceled the power of Lenin's words that had mesmerized the masses into a mindless trance-like state. We broke the power of any unseen ley-lines that allowed demonic access to and from other parts of the city. Then with heads bowed, we asked the Lord Jesus to reveal to the Latvians the truth of the gospel message.

With an explosion of joy in our hearts, after identifying the last power point we victoriously marched down the city square singing the well-known worship chorus, "Shine Jesus Shine."

In the center of the city square stands a towering statue called the "Freedom Statue." This was the one statue that the Soviets did not destroy during their occupation. As we marched by this magnificent symbol of freedom, we shouted: *"Let freedom come to Latvia through Christ."*

Special note: The next day there were two Latvian soldiers standing guard in front of the Freedom Statue. Until this writing, they have continued to *guard the freedom*. A missionary from our church wrote, "Two days after you left, huge signs appeared along the sidewalk between the flower market and the Freedom Statue, where we walked and sang after making our pronouncement. Each letter is on a sign and together they spell the phrase, 'GOD BLESS LATVIA!' We're watching for more signs!"

There were three power points I had seen in my dream. We had identified Lenin's statue and the old castle of bondage. The last one in my dream was something called "Satan." As we stood on the concrete where the Lenin statute once stood, I pointed to my left and commented, "The last power point is this direction."

With us was Latvian-born Maija Krista. I asked, "Maija, where is a place called "Satan" that you feel the devil has claimed Latvia for himself?"
She answered, "Oh, it must be Satan's Lake! The lake is very beautiful and around the lake are thousands of apartments."

"Oh, my," I said, "that's it... let's go!" A couple of hours later, the five of us piled into the missionary's car.

Once at the lake, the team sensed this was indeed the third power point, the one that had been a mystery to me. We inched out of the warm car and into the cold wind and blowing snow. We stood on the elevated side of the embankment and looked out across the lake.

Satan's Lake (Devil's Lake) in summer. Riga, Latvia

It was frozen—solid. Strangely, dozens of blackbirds stood on the icy surface in the center of the lake. This was a mandate from the Lord I thought, so we lined up beside each other to face the lake. Very quietly each of the team members prayed or read Scripture. Then I asked Maija, our Latvian native, to repent on behalf of her people who had dedicated the lake to Satan.

As she did, she began to weep which stirred us all. Our hearts were broken for the bondage of the Latvian people, who were so sad and fearful. Now it was my turn to pray.

"Father, Scripture says, in Psalms 24:1 that *'That the earth is the Lord's, and everything in it, the world and all who live in it.'* However, your archenemy, Satan, has come into this area as a squatter. (A squatter is a person who illegally sets up camp on another's property and acts as the legal owner.) Father, we ask your permission and special anointing to remove the squatter from this lake and return it to you, its rightful owner. I ask you, Lord Jesus, to put a ring of fire around this lake as a testimony to us that you have spoiled the devil's plan." Each team member nodded in agreement that God would have us proceed with direct spiritual warfare.

I reminded each team member to open their eyes as we continued. (Never close your eyes when you confront spiritual darkness. And the only reason I addressed Satan is because the lake bore his name.) I firmly spoke, "Satan, in the powerful name of Jesus Christ our Lord, we command you to leave this lake. You can't have the people of this region. You have been exposed and delivered to us by Almighty God. Together, we send you an eviction notice and declare this lake is NOT yours. You are defeated. Leave NOW!"

The moment I finished, the blackbirds in the middle of the lake, as though mysteriously frightened, squawked and flew away. Next, we watched in awe as a remarkable thing occurred! Around the outer edge of the frozen lake, the ice rapidly began to melt inwardly even though the temperature was in the teens. We couldn't believe our eyes. Even those walking around the lake stopped and stared in amazement. Our team watched and praised God as the lake melted to about five feet in. Remarkably, as we continued to watch, we could see cracks form throughout the lake and a green substance bubble up between the cracks in the ice. We were amazed! Our team was confident that God had taken back the ownership of His Lake. Excited we left to go back and share the miracles we had seen that day.

To this day we do not know for *certain* what the green substance oozing up between the cracks might have been. About a year later, I was teaching in a farming community in central Texas. I had shared this story with the congregation explaining that we weren't sure what the green algae 'junk' meant. At the break, several farmers approached me to share that in the spring of each year, a lake will "turn over." They explained this is a purifying process as the algae in the water will resettle. The farmers were confident that we had seen Satan's Lake *turn over*. Well glory to God! That day, not in the spring, but in the bitterly cold and snowy winter, the devil's lake in Riga, Latvia *turned over* as our prayer team declared aloud its new name. We renamed the lake, "Lake Jehovah!"

The entire U.S. team and the Latvian nationals celebrated in the belief that God was laying a new foundation in the newly independent nation of Latvia. Since our time there in the early 90s, new churches have been planted and the gospel is regularly shared.

Evangelism and extending His Kingdom is the purpose!

Since before creating the world (1 Peter 1:20-21), God wants to be known by us. His deepest purpose is for all to come to know Him through salvation (1 Timothy 2:4). The purposes of discerning the climate of our cities are to research historical information, seek God for revelation, recognize and dismantle the hindrances brought by sin, and then believe Him for a visible indication that something has happened. Pray, pray, pray expectantly for lives to be altered and celebrate exuberantly every move of God that follows.

What are you waiting for? Put down this book. *Get started today!*

NOTES:

[1] Alice Smith, *Delivering the Captives* (Minneapolis, Bethany House), 2006, p. 32-33.
[2] *Spain's New Territory*, pp.2-4.
[3] Ibid.
[4] James M. Day, *The Gulf Coast Cannibals "The Karankawas,"* pp.72-73.
[5] *The Gulf Coast Cannibals*, p. 80.
[6] Ibid. pp. 82-83.
[7] Alfred Watkins, *The Old Straight Track*, (Abacus Publishers, England), 1925.
[8] George Otis, Jr. Spiritual Mapping Field Guide: Glossary of Related Terms, The Sentinel Group, 1994, p.4.
[9] Ieva Vitina, *Old Riga Tourist Guide* (Spriditis, Riga 1992), p.7.
[10] Ibid.

www.ingramcontent.com/pod-product-compliance
Lightning Source LLC
Chambersburg PA
CBHW032050290426
44110CB00012B/1029